JESUS

YOU SHALL LOVE YOUR NEIGHBOR AS YOURSELF

IN THE BEGINING WAS THE WORD, AND THE WORD WAS WITH GOD

Great Names
JESUS

AND THE WORD WAS GOD

IN THE SIXTH MONTH THE ANGEL GABRIEL WAS SENT FROM GOD TO A SITY OF GALI

NAZARETH

Jesus was one of the greatest holy men who ever lived. During his lifetime, he worked tirelessly to teach people about love and the true meaning of life. And for nearly 2,000 years, his message has flourished and spread across the entire world.

According to historical records, Jesus may have lived for only 33 years. However, his short life has had a far-reaching influence on the history of the world. In the days when Jesus lived, knowledge was passed on by word of mouth. People heard things, remembered them, and told them to others, generation after generation. The stories passed down about Jesus are full of mysterious and miraculous events. Whether these events are entirely true or not is not important. The important thing is to understand the eternal truths that lie at the heart of these stories.

Around 4 B.C., in the town of Nazareth, in what is now the country of Israel, there lived a carpenter, Joseph, and his wife Mary. Before Mary and Joseph were married, an angel appeared to

AND ALL WENT TO BE ENROLED EACH T

Mary. The angel told Mary she would bear a son who would lead his people to salvation.

All the four Gospels record the life of Jesus, but only Mark and Luke mention his birth. In John, there is an explanation for why the Son of God became a man: "In the beginning was the Word. . . . The Word became flesh and came to live among us . . . full of grace and truth."

Obeying a tax law, Joseph and Mary arrived in Bethlehem. The inns of the city were full. The couple could not find a room anywhere. Mary was about to give birth to her child. Finally, a kindhearted person took the couple to an old stable and made them a bed in one corner. Jesus was born in that stable. Months after his birth, a group of Persian astronomers, dressed in fine robes and carrying many treasures, arrived to worship the child. They had seen an extraordinarily bright star that suddenly had appeared in the skies above Bethlehem. These wise men followed the star to the home of Jesus. When they saw the child, they rejoiced. They gave him gold, frankincense, and myrrh. News of their visit spread quickly. But if the birth of Jesus prompted some people to rejoice, it caused

...SAW THE CHILD WITH MARY HIS MOTHER, AND THEY FELL DOWN AND WORSHIP[PED] HIM...

...HE ROS...AND TOOK THE CHILD AND HIS MOTHER BY NIGHT, AND DEPARTED TO EGYPT.

at least one person to worry. That person was the powerful King Herod.

Jewish history was a constant cycle of exile, war, and oppression. The Jews were ruled by one conqueror after another, and they longed for the Messiah to come and save them. Messiah is a Hebrew word for "annointed or chosen one."

King Herod was a cruel and treacherous man. He became king by killing and lying. He did not care about people or God. He cared only about keeping his Roman bosses happy. The Romans occupied many lands. They built a great empire but did not rule all of it directly. Sometimes they used "puppets," like King Herod, to rule for them. The puppet rulers appeared to be in charge, but the real power remained with the Roman governors.

King Herod was old and sick. He was frightened and suspicious. When he heard about the birth of a miracle child who might become king, he grew terrified. He ordered his men to go to Bethlehem and murder every male child under the age of three. Herod did not want anyone claiming his throne.

The Bible says that before Herod ordered the baby boys to be killed, Joseph had a dream. In the dream, an angel said to him: "Get up!

RACHEL WEEPING FOR HER CHILD

ISTENING TO THEM AND ASKING TH

Take the child and his mother and flee to Egypt. Remain there until I tell you!" Joseph obeyed.

A year later, King Herod died. The slaughter of the children came to an end. Joseph and Mary returned to Nazareth with their child. Joseph went back to work as a carpenter.

There is one story in the Bible about Jesus' early years. This story tells about Joseph and Mary finding the 12-year-old discussing religion with the priests in Jerusalem. From this story, we can see that he must have been a very clever child, for he did not have any formal religious training.

One of the first people to influence Jesus was his cousin, John the Baptist. John wore rough clothes made of camel hair. He lived alone in the wilderness, where he ate dried locusts and wild honey. John would wave his arms at people, and toss his long, tangled hair and beard. "Repent! Repent!" he urged. "The Kingdom of Heaven is at hand!"

More and more people came to hear John the Baptist preach. They wanted to repent of their sins. John helped them wash away their sins by baptizing them with river water. Jesus was moved by John's work. Jesus asked

US CAME FROM NAZARETH OF GALILEE AND WAS BAPTIZED BY JOHN IN THE JORDAN

John to baptize him. Then Jesus went into the wilderness to listen to the Holy Spirit in solitude.

Alone in the wilderness, Jesus thought and prayed. After 40 days, the devil appeared to Jesus. The devil tried to tempt Jesus. The devil said: "If you are the Son of God, tell this stone to become bread." Jesus answered quietly. "It is written: Human beings shall not live by bread alone, but by the word of God."

Jesus returned from the wilderness. He knew that his beliefs were very different from the religion and practices of the time, especially his understanding of love. Jesus also knew that it was time to leave home and travel, to teach people about love, mercy, tolerance, and forgiveness. He was now 30 years old. More than a carpenter's son, he was also the Son of God.

Wherever Jesus went, people came to hear him speak. Jesus taught that God was patient and loving, the father of all creation. People came to hear Jesus' message and see his miracles. One day, for example, Jesus was at a wedding when the wine ran out. Jesus ordered the servants to fill the serving vessels with water, and then serve the guests. When the guests drank, they were amazed to find that the water had become wine.

OR FORTY DAYS IN THE WILDERNESS TEMPTE

HIS, THE FIRST OF HIS SINS, JESUS DID AT CA'NA IN GALILE. AND HIS DISCIPLES BELIEVED IN H

BLESSED ARE YOU POOR, FOR YOURS IS THE KINGDOM OF GOD.

Jesus was not interested in politics. He did not concern himself with who was in charge of the nation, nor did he teach Greek philosophy or Roman law. In his heart there was only love. He loved his friends and relatives, and all the people of the world.

The most important sermon Jesus gave was the famous Sermon on the Mount. In that sermon, he said: "Blessed are the humble, for theirs is the Kingdom of heaven. Blessed are those who mourn, for they shall be comforted. Blessed are the meek, for they will inherit the Earth. Blessed are those who hunger and thirst for righteousness, for they shall be satisfied. Blessed are the merciful, for they shall obtain mercy. Blessed are the pure of heart, for they shall see God."

Jesus also said: "You are the light of the world. Don't hide your goodness, but let it shine like a candle in a dark room. We don't light candles and put them under the table. We put them up high to shed light on all. The old teachings say, 'an eye for an eye, a tooth for a tooth.' But I say, if someone hits you on the right cheek, then turn the other cheek. Love your enemies, and pray for those who persecute you."

JESUS THEN TOOK THE LOAVES, AND WHE[N]

Jesus had 12 disciples to help him. In one story, Jesus and his disciples were crossing a lake by boat. A great storm began to blow. Waves crashed over the boat. The disciples cried out for Jesus to save them.

"Why are you afraid?" Jesus asked. "Don't you have faith?" He lifted his hand and called out to the wind and waves. Immediately, everything became calm.

Another time, the disciples were caught in another storm at sea. Jesus came to them, walking atop the water. One of the disciples, Peter, shouted, "Lord, if it is you, command me to come to you on the water." Jesus answered: "Come!" Peter got out of the boat. He took several steps on the water, but then became frightened and began to sink. Jesus reached out and caught him. "You of little faith," Jesus said. "Why did you doubt?"

Another day, Jesus was leading his disciples up a high mountain to pray. Suddenly, a bright cloud appeared in the sky. A voice rang out: "This is my beloved son, with whom I am well pleased. Listen to him!" The disciples fell to the ground in awe. Jesus tapped them on the shoulders. "Rise," he said, "and have no fear."

ND IN THE F   TH WATCH OF THE   HE   ML

IS IS MY BELOVED SON, WITH WHOM I AM WELL PLEASED, LISTEN TO HIM

Jesus was good, honest, and loving. People trusted him. He comforted the sick and the wounded; he also healed their bodies. His ability to cure the sick drew many people to him. People of many races and from many lands came to be healed by Jesus. He did not care if they were male or female; rich or poor; Jew or non-Jew; saint or sinner. He loved them all.

Once, two blind beggars who were sitting by the road heard that Jesus was passing. They called out to him: "Lord, have mercy on us!" The crowd told them to be quiet, but they continued to cry out. Jesus went over to the beggars. "What do you want me to do for you?" he asked. "Lord, open our eyes!" they said. Jesus gently touched their eyes—and they could see.

Once, some women begged him to touch their children and pray for them. The disciples wanted to send the women away. "Our Lord is in a hurry," the disciples said. "He does not have much time." But Jesus said: "Let the children come to me. Do not stop them, for the Kingdom of Heaven belongs to such as these." Jesus placed his hands on the children and said: "Those who are not like children will never enter the Kingdom of Heaven."

HEN HOW WERE YOUR EYES OPENE?

RMIT YOUR CHILDREN TO COME TO M AND DON'T PROHIBIT THE BECAU

FEAR NOT, DAUGHTER OF ZION; BEHOLD, YOUR KING IS COMING, SITTING UPON AN ASS'S COLT

Jesus taught that God loved all races and all classes, regardless of whether they were rich or poor. His teachings made him very popular. To the authorities, this made Jesus seem dangerous. Shortly before the Jewish holiday of Passover, Jesus rode into Jerusalem on a donkey. A large crowd greeted him.

They laid palm fronds on the road leading into town. People followed Jesus into the city, singing songs of praise. This worried the leaders even more. The government leaders were afraid that Jesus was so popular he would start a rebellion against Rome. The Jewish leaders feared that if Jesus did start a rebellion, Rome would destroy the Jews. The Jewish authorities also did not like the fact that Jesus spoke of himself as being equal to God. After he arrived in Jerusalem, Jesus went into the Jewish temple. He was shocked at what he saw. The house of worship had been turned into a market. In every corner, merchants sold animals, or exchanged money. Jesus was furious! He shouted angrily: "God's temple is a place of prayer, not a marketplace!" He picked up a whip and drove the merchants out of the temple.

A HOUSE OF PRAYER; BUT YOU MAKE IT A DEN

HEY PAID HIM THIRTY PIECES OF SILVER

Jesus knew that it might be dangerous for him to go to Jerusalem. But he wanted to celebrate Passover there so he went anyway. The authorities decided to arrest Jesus. They wanted to capture him in a manner that would not anger the people. Jesus had a disciple named Judas. Judas may have loved God and Jesus, but he loved money more. One night, Judas slipped out and went to the high priests, who wanted to arrest Jesus. "If you want Jesus, I can deliver him for you." The overjoyed priests paid Judas 30 pieces of silver.

The night before Jesus was caught, he had supper with his disciples. This was the famous Last Supper. Jesus knew he was in danger, but he remained calm. He gently washed the feet of all his disciples. He urged them to follow his example in all things. Then he picked up a loaf of bread. He broke off a piece for each disciple. "Take this," he said. "It is my body, which is given for you." He passed around a cup of wine. "Drink," he said. "This is the blood I shed for the world."

A NEW COMMANDMENT I GIVE TO YOU, THAT YOU LOVE ANOTHER; EVEN AS I HAVE LO

AND HE CAME UP TO JESUS AT ONCE AND SAID, "HAIL, MASTER!" AND HE KISSED HIM

After supper, Jesus led his disciples into the gardens at Gethsemene, to pray. His heart was very troubled. Jesus prayed to God: "My Father, if it be possible, take this suffering from me. But do not do as I wish; do only as you wish." Soon a large group of armed men burst into the gardens. They surrounded Jesus and his disciples. Judas walked up to Jesus and kissed him on the cheek. This was his signal. The soldiers grabbed Jesus. Another disciple, Peter, drew his sword. Jesus stopped him. "Put your sword away," Jesus said. "If I need protection, my Father will protect me." Jesus went calmly while the disciples fled. Jesus was taken to the authorities for questioning. He gave no answers to their questions. He said nothing. The authorities took Jesus to the Roman governor, Pilate.

Pilate did not know what to do with Jesus, so he asked King Herod to decide. Herod refused. By this time, a crowd had gathered. The mob began to shout: "Crucify him!" "Crucify him!" So Jesus was sentenced to die on the cross.

THEY CRIED OUT AGAIN, "CRUCIFY HIM!"

The soldiers dressed Jesus in a dirty old robe. They placed a crown of thorns on his head. They ordered him to pick up a cross and carry it to the execution ground. Jesus was weak and very tired. He dragged himself slowly up the hill. The heavy cross was on his back. The soldiers whipped Jesus repeatedly. Each step was more difficult than the last.

Time and again, Jesus fell, but he always staggered back to his feet. The path was lined with people who watched the innocent, loving man as he walked to his death. Some cried out for Jesus to be let go, but their cries came too late. Jesus was nailed to the cross. He died slowly and painfully. With his last breath, he prayed: "My Father, forgive them, for they do not know what they have done."

O THEY TOOK JE US, AND HE WENT OUT

AND IT WAS THE THIRD HOUR, WHEN THEY CRUCIFIED HIM

A man named Joseph asked Pilate if he could have Jesus' body. Pilate agreed. Joseph took the body down from the cross. He wrapped the body in a linen cloth and placed it inside a tomb that had been cut into a rock. On the morning of the third day, three women went to the tomb. They planned to annoint the body with spices. But the stone in front of the tomb had been rolled away. The body was gone!

All that remained were the linen wrappings. Inside the tomb stood a man in dazzling white clothing. "Don't be afraid," the man said to the women. "The one you are looking for is not here. He has risen and lives again." The news quickly spread that Jesus had risen from the dead. One of the disciples, Thomas, did not believe the story. One day, Jesus appeared to him. "Thomas, why do you doubt?" Jesus asked. "Look at my hands and feet. Touch me and believe."

VE YOU BELIEVED BECAUSE YOU HAVE SEEN ME? BLESSED ARE THOSE WHO HAVE NOT SEEN AND

TEACHIN[G] [T]O OBSERVE ALL THA[T I] HAVE COMMANDED YOU; AND LO, I A[M]

After Jesus died, the disciples continued to spread the message of love. Jesus brought love, forgiveness, hope, and justice into our lives. He showed us how we should live.

From him, we know that life and love will last forever, for God's love is more powerful than death.

WITH YOU ALWAYS, TO THE CLOSE OF THE A

Mason Crest Publishers, Inc.
370 Reed Road
Broomall, Pennsylvania 19008
866-MCP-BOOK toll free

Illustrations copyright © 1999 Alexander Mikhnushev
Published in association with Grimm Press Ltd., Taiwan

1 3 5 7 9 8 6 4 2

Library of Congress Cataloging-in-Publication Data:

on file at the Library of Congress.

ISBN 1-59084-138-7
ISBN 1-59084-133-6 series